Till MY LAST BREATH

Atul Gore

Qurate
qaratebooks.com

Till My Last Breath
Atul Gore

Published by Qurate Books Pvt. Ltd.

First Published in 2022

ISBN: 978-93-94600-47-8

Qurate
qratebooks.com

Qurate Books Pvt. Ltd.
Goa 403623, India
www.quratebooks.com
Tel: 18002106527, Email: info@quratebooks.com

Ask a craftsman which is his favorite work. Ask a mother who is her favorite child.

When asked these questions, all you can do is smile. Nothing else. Something similar happened to me while working with Mr. Gore on his book.

Having written a few books, while working on this book, I was mesmerized. I could feel the pain and experience the journey that he has gone through. Only a person with his mettle could have handled it. I give credit to a large extent to his upbringing and the values ingrained by his parents in him.

In many of the conversations we had while working on his project, every time he narrated an example or a case study from the past in which he had helped someone, his eyes had that sparkle as if it just happened a few days back. He loves helping others unconditionally. While he never mentioned to me but I'm sure if even today someone walks to him and says he needs help in his personal or professional life, Mr. Gore will not hesitate to say a yes, even without discussing the commercials. He has so much to give.

The commitment and discipline he showed in the making of this book is commendable. Despite his busy schedule, he was always available for the video sessions we conducted to capture his mind. He was always prompt to approve the drafts with minimum fuss. I don't think we would have got this clarity to work on this book without such involvement and dedication from him. His warmth and gentleness is contagious.

It was an absolute delight to work on this project. We take great pride in being associated with the creation of this book.

The journey will continue as the world needs more from him.

Wishing him all the very best.

Rajnish G Shirsat

Book Creation Services – BookMark

rajnish@rsenterprises.info

Foreword

In our day-to-day life, we often meet strangers. We meet them at business shows, a shop, airports and many such places and never know what connection we may have with them. A small conversation can lead to lasting relationships. My story with the author, Mr. Gore, was no different.

I met Mr. Gore in 1997 when things needed to be more settled with me personally and professionally. My late husband, Shri Mannoj Rijhwaani, and I used to have constant quarrels. There were issues regarding money matters, and our standard of living. Our kid was also very small then. Those were the days when we were under a lot of stress.

The author and I had a common friend Lazarus Dias (Today a very successful insurance trainer, coach, and author) who had invited my husband and me way back in 1997 for a training session led by Mr. Gore. While I was reluctant to visit as that was increasing our expenses, my husband insisted that we attend. Mannoj came back and told me that his counselling with Mr. Gore was incomplete. He wanted me to see Mr. Gore so that same can be brought to its conclusion. I was not keen to participate but agreed, as I didn't want my husband's work to be affected. The first thought that came to my mind was, what kind of counselling he was going to provide when he also would be facing some challenges in his own life. I was not convinced about a session with Mr. Gore at all, but as the conversation went on, I found my answers from him. His knowledge and experience were impressive. He himself had gone through a lot in his life but had come out of every challenge. I remember he told me to confide in everything and empty all my thoughts, which was a big relief. My journey with Mr. Gore had begun.

Mr. Gore's biggest strength is to connect with people very quickly. He is a good listener and allows people to talk. We often give our problems to him and he comes up with possible solutions. He likes to guide us in these challenging situations with his experience and helps us find the best way forward. He will put up all options in front of you and ask you to choose and implement them. His suggestions are never forced on us, which gives us the freedom to make our own decisions. He will never be demanding, but his experience and presence are commanding.

His most significant teaching has been from the book "7 Habits of Highly Effective People" by Dr. Stephen R Covey and the Kaizen techniques. Having been associated with him all these years and being a part of his sessions as a participant, a Group Assistant, and attending his counselling sessions as an observer, these teachings have been ingrained into my system.

I need to mention one incident that cemented our bonding. As I was going through a lot of difficulties running my other business of a boutique, while Mannoj was offering financial planning to clients, I started a boutique and had to deal with workers and semi-skilled people who were part of my team. This group of people troubled me with their constant demands of advance salaries and issues at work, and I used to be very liberal with them. Still, when it came to delivering work at peak times or during seasonal requirements, they did not respond to my needs at all. All this was disturbing me, and I consulted Mr. Gore. A brief talk with him made me realize my mistakes and the possible solutions. I could correct myself going forward. He told me I shouldn't be falling prey to their constant requests, not everytime. While we choose to be understanding and show empathy, it doesn't always work like that. He told me to draw a line and this helped. Such was the soothing impact of Mr. Gore on me. These are extraordinary skills that very few can be proud of.

Another incident was when my nephew Yash, was in two minds after passing his CA exams on the way forward in his career. His big dilemma was choosing between returning to New Delhi or continuing work with Mannoj in Thane. Again, just one session with Mr. Gore and Yash could evaluate the options with him and arrive at his decision(choosing Thane as the place of work & stay). Today, he is extremely happy with the decision made and is doing well. This may sound very simple, but the situation was tough than it appeared, and we were pleased that we found the right way ahead with Mr. Gore's help.

After Mannoj, my husband passed away, I had to take up the responsibility of running our mutual fund financial planning business. With so many families and their hard-earned money entrusted to us, I had no option but to take charge. While my nephew Yash and my son Rahuul would lead the business in the future, in the short term, I had to set things in motion. I have a great staff to support. But I realized it is very tough to fill in the shoes of Mannoj. My husband was friendly and cheerful and would get the work done easily, as the staff greatly loved him. I have my way of working and appear to be demanding and bossy. The situation, I realized, had to be addressed and made workable. Hence, who else but to get Mr. Gore again on Board as our anchor, counsellor and trainer? As domain expert he may not contribute to our business directly, but as a counsellor and trainer with long experience, he can put my staff at ease. He is friendly, and my staff loves him too. The work environment has improved, and the team can confide with him, too, which helps our business in return to normalize and again growing.

Life has come back full circle for me.I started my business journey with Mr. Gore, and today, in my most delicate time when my husband is not around, I have a friend, philosopher, and guide in Mr. Gore with me.

I'm sure readers of this book will take a lot of inspiration from this story. Students will understand the importance of grit and determination, the essence of the 7 Habits, its practices and values promoted by the book. The MSME owners will know how to scale up their business and learn from him the planning process. Professionals and individuals, whether in industry or otherwise, will find in him a person who is always ready to guide and give back to them.

In conclusion, I would like to say, the world gets empowered when there are people like him around.

Best Wishes

Sangitaa M Rijhwaani
Director
Rijhwaani Associates

Preface

Writing a book has been on my mind for some time. I didn't know the wait would have been so long, but as they say, you must wait for the right time.

Things need to fall in place, most crucially from a time perspective. We get so entangled in our day-to-day activities that we often skip certain milestones we want to achieve or reach. Writing a book was one of them. People around you often observe you, get inspired, appreciate your work and want you to reach a larger audience which motivates you. This was happening with me for some time until Mrs Sangitaa Rijhwani, Director, Rijhwaani Associates LLP, proposed this, put her foot down and insisted I begin somewhere. Thank you, Sangitaaji. I'm indeed very grateful to you. It finally took shape, and everything started to roll appropriately.

The "Why" behind writing this book can be summarized in a few words. Sharing my experience and guiding people is the foundation of this book. Still, the most crucial element is to inspire many like me who were initially not seasoned consultants or trainers to come forward and take this path. There's so much to share, and there are so many qualified and experienced people out there who, if they can step into a consultant's or trainer's shoes, can help many people hungry for knowledge. I hope this book reaches out to these people, makes them enter this rewarding and fulfilling industry, and enables them to transform people. The satisfaction and joy at the end of your consulting cannot be measured in terms of value. The day you walk out of your client's office with a written testimonial or hear your client telling others how you helped and transformed them, you will realize the importance of your work delivered.

My exposure to this wonderful world of consulting, training, counselling and coaching started when I worked closely with insurance agents and their Development Officers. My association with them continued for a few years until I got the opportunity to get associated with the world of MSMEs (Micro, Small and Medium Enterprises). In India, MSMEs contribute nearly 8% of the country's GDP, around 45% of the manufacturing output, and approximately 40% of the country's exports. It won't be wrong to refer to them as the 'Backbone of the country.' MSMEs are an important sector of the global economy and have contributed immensely to their respective country's socio-economic development. It generates employment opportunities and works hand-in-hand toward developing the nation's backward and rural areas. According to the annual report by the Government (2018-19), there are around 6,08,41,245 MSMEs in India. If you add the unorganized sector, which is considerably big in our country, along with the MSMEs, the numbers can be further mindboggling.

A typical profile of an entrepreneur or a business owner in the MSME is not very different. Most of them have been average students and back-benchers but were always street-smart, hard-working and had that fire in the belly. The MSME owners are unsung heroes as there are phenomenal success stories of many but very few have heard of them. They are never in the limelight and have built over a period of time, massive enterprises. They start their businesses sometimes by accident, sometimes by a plan and many times as a family tradition. Before they realize it, they taste success, sometimes by chance or most of the time by some opportunity which walked into their lap, through a reference. This goes on for a few years till they hit a plateau. Typically, reaching this plateau takes a couple of years for a few or can be even ten years. Unfortunately, the MSMEs die early if they do not adapt to proven management practices or take professional guidance.

When they hit this plateau, the critical question is, "How do I scale further"? That is where consultants come in. Not all understand the need to get professional help, but these are logical steps they need to take. Marshall Goldsmith's book "What Got You Here, Won't Get You There" explains this. He says, "Your hard work is paying off. You are doing well in your field. But something is standing between you and the next level of achievement. Perhaps one minor flaw–a behaviour you barely even recognize–is the only thing keeping you from where you want to be. I work primarily to uncover this aspect and have shared it in this book.

This book also expresses my gratitude towards my elder brother Dr Anil Gore, PhD from Kentucky University, U.S. He is my role model who has been instrumental in helping me grow and overcome many challenges.

My mentor, A. P. Remedios, a Graduate Engineer from the UK, he worked in Zimbabwe and finally settled in India. It was he who taught me engineering in the most appropriate manner beyond what a book could explain to me.

Father Orlando Rodrigues from Father Agnel Engineering College - It was he who established the entire Vashi complex spread over 15 Acres land of English, Marathi Medium Schools, Polytechnic, Engineering college ITI, Production unit, Orphanage, Hostel (both gender) Business school, Sports Academy). I learned the administrative aspects from him especially in running larger establishments.

Avinash Gore –a Mechanical Engineer, MBA (MKT) who Started his career with Alfa Laval, worked in India, Australia, Europe, U.S. and Retired as President of U.S Co, also a Member Hoganas Board. He taught me the basics of management.

Finally, Ferdie D'Souza - who established Landmark in India and then settled in the UK. He has been my role model as Trainer.

I also want to thank two significant institutions that gave me the platform to excel in my field. "LAKSHYAVEDH Institute of Leadership & Excellence, which has been highly active in Personal and Professional Development Training since January 2008.

The other institution that left a lasting impact on my career is Zig Ziglar. Ziglar is specialized in Personal Development Training, Providing Coaching for Presentation Skills, Sales, Small Business Owners, Speakers and much more. Their specialized courses namely, Ziglar Strategies for Success, Ziglar Sales Process and Ziglar Train the Trainer are a master class. It is a US-based institution with offices all across the world. I was fortunate to have visited Hong Kong for certification courses of Zig Ziglar, namely, the "Certified Strategies of Success."At Ziglar, inspiring people is what they do. They are the leading provider of training that helps people achieve the best in personal and vocational performance. The most outstanding and stand-out aspect of

Ziglar has been the way they redefined "Sales" making the function doable by anyone. He simplified Sales so much that everyone could believe they achieve outstanding success in it as a profession. Zig Ziglar, America's most influential and beloved encourager and believer that everyone could be, do and have more, founded the Zig Ziglar Corporation in 1977. He influenced an estimated quarter of a billion individuals through his 33 books, including the bestseller See You at the Top, which has sold almost two million copies. Today Zig's son Tom leads Ziglar in its efforts to continue to deliver his father's inspirational message to high-achievers around the world.

Today, I'm probably in the best zone of my life. My consulting, coaching, training and mentoring business is doing well beyond my imagination. I never planned to operate in this domain and enjoy it so much. The joy of helping others and sharing my experience and wisdom are soothing my bruises.

About the Author

"Don't judge people, you never know what battle they are fighting"

Unknown

It is easy to pass judgements. The shine behind a diamond sparkle is earned after what it has gone through, which we don't see. We don't see or witness the pain, the agony, or the mental battle that an athlete goes through.--

Mine was a no different story.

My roots are from Wai, also known as Viraatnagari. It was believed that the Pandavas stayed with King Viraat of Wai while in exile. An important centre for business and commerce with traders heading towards Satara and Kolhapur or the port of Konkan. At 35 km from the city of Satara, Wai is truly a pilgrim town with almost 100 temples. Most of them are constructed in the Hemadpanthi style, which uses colossal stone slabs without mortar. Though amid this beautiful place, my life was always in turbulence.

I grew up as an unwanted child in my mother's womb. I opened my eyes a month later than it usually takes to be born. When family planning was not a concept or topic of discussion, my mother was carrying me but had already started taking measures to ensure another child was not born to her. Besides damaging her health, the unusual precautions took their toll and affected my health when I was in her womb. I was born with dark skin and was unhealthy, but fortunately, my health improved after I reached the age of twelve.

To a great extent, my over-enterprising father's DNA was responsible for my grooming, which, time and again, reflected in the kind of actions even I took. While my father was over-ambitious and restless but had an honest desire to grow in life and on the other hand, my mother used to ground him for his actions. His repeated business ventures failed, which did play their part in the family. Though a Diploma holder in Civil Engineering, my father was always in awe of someone holding a Degree. He worked initially in the irrigation department and subsequently joined MSRTC for good and always carried a complex when he came across someone having a degree. His job demanded transfers across Maharashtra, and the family travelled with him. I ended up studying at six schools and four colleges by the time I finished my education.

I grew up in a family of four siblings, each having earned a space but not me. My fragile health was always a topic of discussion, a worry for all. A constant mention of this affected my thinking as I grew up and laid the foundation of my self-doubt and indecisiveness or hesitant nature to believe in my ability. My eldest brother was a genius and was called a "pandit" next was my sister, who was always pampered the most by my father, and I was the third child. Everyone in my family was never sure of my abilities, primarily because of my health. A constant worry and expression of doubt were related to me, which affected my confidence. I used to crave attention and recognition.

As years passed by, I started doing well in my studies. I was a topper in college and 4th at university. After passing from prestigious VJTI as 1st class graduate engineer, my father asked me to join his government of Maharashtra undertaking MSRTC. He wanted to prove a point to many and brag about his son being a degree holder. Today, when I think it over, I feel good that I could fulfill his dream. Then came a turning point when I was told by my father to start a business in construction. He used to advise me, which I never liked as he had proved he was not a successful businessman in the past. My perfectionist attitude was also a hindrance to our business growth, and eventually, it was a disastrous end.

My confidence was shaken due to this failed entrepreneurial venture, which escalated on a personal front when I started losing my hair. The baldness gave me further complexity, primarily due to the damage done when I was in my mother's womb. As age caught up, maybe the falling immunity also affected my health and this baldness. A sense of insecurity crept in, and I constantly struggled with myself in this period. Before I thought it was too late, I thought of getting married.

My marriage and the period ahead have been one traumatic period of my life. It is full of complexities. My wife, a very well-educated lady (BTech), then completed her Ph.D. in

Engineering from IIT Mumbai, and our thinking was ahead of our times. Besides planning for a biological child, we thought of adopting a girl child. My wife was very adamant and didn't want to get entangled in the usual grooming and nurturing of children and wanted to adopt a grown-up child, not an infant, to which I agreed.

Family life was full of stress and strain. My wife and I used to quarrel constantly and never got along. The adopted child proved to be a wrong decision as I used to hear about her inactions, misbehavior, and wild nature. It reached a stage when our quarrels and constant unrest at home got to a point where not once but thrice when we came to file for a divorce.

As years passed, I also learned that the root cause of this stress, particularly between my wife and me, was our nature and emotional quotient. We were poles apart, as expressed by Dr Rajendra Barve, a psychiatrist, friend, and relative who told me this. His advice was either I live with this or exit, and I walked out of my wife's life by handing over everything I had as my asset. My adopted daughter Sonali accompanied me, but even her life took an unexpected turn due to strained marriage life, and she deserted me. Today, I live happily alone.

Even though nothing was planned during these emotional storms, my professional life was taking shape. God had different plans and was opening doors for me unknown.

A cousin brother of mine gifted me a book named "7 Habits of Highly Effective People" by Stephen Covey. I read the book, and that changed me forever. One important lesson from that book is when the author says, after reading something, always teach the same to others within forty-eight hours. He said, to understand, you have to teach, and I started doing that in my own way. Friends and people around me started liking my preaching and teaching style. Doors began opening to consult and train companies in the engineering and insurance industries. The insurance industry was a significant turning point as my student got recognition at LIRT (Life Insurance Round Table), equivalent to the US MDRT. Group coaching opportunities emerged from there, and I started customizing courses. There was no looking back then.

Once I learned an important lesson from a friend who runs an NGO. I was telling her that after all that I did in my life, there was no gratitude shown to me by anyone. My adopted daughter also deserted me in the end; my biological daughter Savitri was so influenced by her mother that we never shared that bonding, and my wife never got along with me. While I was feeling victimized, this friend told me that she had helped more than one thousand girls in her life, but no one turned back to thank her. She ridiculed my thought process and told me to look ahead and help others. This statement of hers showed me the way to move forward.

Today, I work as a trainer, counsellor, consultant and mentor. Somewhere I feel, not just because of my experience and age, I have seen it all personally and professionally, that I can step into anyone's shoes to understand what they are going through. I bring calmness and pause to many who go through emotional, physical or even spiritual imbalance, whether in their personal or professional life.

A ship is the safest when anchored, but it is not the place where it is meant to be always. One needs to face the battles and look into the eyes of the problems you come across.

No one knows this better than I do.

Atul Gore

apggmc@gmail.com.

Table of Content

Instructions for using this book.

This book is to be used as a reference manual (to be referred to occasionally) by counselees, counsellors, trainers & entrepreneurs. At end of each chapter there are questions, please write the answers using pencil because over a period your answers may change. Please do not read it as a novel or storybook.

How do you charge for your services Mr. Gore?

"Price is what you pay, Value is what you get"

Warren Buffett

I value my time the most, and the charges reflect around this. The more I'm required to visit a client, the more they spend on me. Money has not been the central aspect of my services. Everyone wants to pay their bills, and so do I, and for that, you need money, but as explained earlier, I came into this profession by chance and started enjoying it. The most significant satisfying part was because I could transform lives. My personal experiences and professional background went into the play, and I could achieve the objectives.

It makes me feel good to mention that seven of the ten proposals I submit get approved, and I'm on board. Knowing the goal posts very clearly matters to me as that simplifies me to know how much time I will spend on every client to show the desired results. Hence, once the time element is known, my charges are communicated.

* *

I came into this profession by chance and started enjoying it. The most significant satisfying part was because I could transform lives.

* *

Questions to the reader:

1. Have you appointed a Consultant, Trainer or a Coach for yourself ever?

   ____

2. What has been your experience?

   ____

3. Were the goal posts defined clearly?

____

4. Were the goals monitored clearly?

____

What is my role as a client? What am I expected to do?

"If you cannot describe what you are doing as a process, you don't know what you are doing"

W. Edwards Deming

When we hit the bull's eye rightly, the client usually wants to jump to this question. What is my role? What is expected from me? How much time will I have to spend on this? Typically, a person wants results and hates a process. I always tell my friends and colleagues jokingly that to get in shape, what if we could send our substitutes to a gym? Will that work? No one likes the pain, the process, the changes, the time to be spent. All we want is a result. Knowing where to hit the hammer is more important than the strength and power of the hit.

My process to achieve results is based on The Theory Of Constraints model.

****

No one likes the pain, the process, the changes, the time to be spent. All we want is a result.

****

The Theory of Constraints is a methodology for identifying the most important limiting factor (i.e., constraint) that stands in the way of achieving a goal and then systematically improving that constraint until it is no longer the limiting factor. In manufacturing, the constraint is often referred to as a bottleneck. The theory of constraints (TOC) is a management philosophy developed by Eliyahu M. Goldratt in his 1984 publication, "The Goal: A Process of Ongoing Improvement." Goldratt suggested that organizations can achieve their goals by identifying and leveraging a system's constraints.

Once appointed, I get to the core. We spend a lot of time understanding the existing systems, processes, dynamics of the organization, industry practices etc. and try to go to the root of the top constraints. Many times, vis-a-vis, what has been briefed to us, the problem lies somewhere else. This needs to be told; one needs to look into its eyes and address it on priority.

* *

Once appointed, I get to the core. We spend a lot of time understanding the existing systems, processes, dynamics of the organization, industry practices etc. and try to go to the root of the top constraints.

* *

As we go along, new constraints emerge, sometimes related or of a less serious nature and sometimes of different nature and types—all these need to be addressed collectively or one by one over a while.

Eventually, what the client gets from me is a process, a system which works long-term.

People with you of less calibre can be managed with appropriate and robust systems, rather than highly qualified people with no systems.

Once this initial groundwork is done, what matters the most is implementation and following the process set in a focused manner. This is what is expected from the client. One has to believe in the process ruthlessly. The results come.

* *

People with you of less calibre can be managed with appropriate and robust systems, rather than highly qualified people with no systems.

* *

Questions to the reader:

1. Do you know what is keeping you awake at night? What is your core constraint?

   ____

2. Which are your top three or five systems set or reporting structure outlined that helps you control and manage your business?

   ____

   ____

3. In which department in your company is your time spent the most and why?

____

____

As our Consultant, will you be responsible for the final results?

"If you focus on results, you will never change. If you focus on change, you will get results"

Jack Dixon

After the initial screening, mainly when it is a fresh client who has heard of us and called for a meeting, this question arises in the client's mind.

A human is tuned to see results. The act or view of before and after always excites everyone. The client often doesn't ask me this question out of respect due to my age but let's accept it; this is a valid question.

During our pitch discussion, I mention that my appointment is your choice, but the exit is mine. Why would I say so? This statement of "exit is mine" speaks volumes of my confidence, belief, and the processes and benchmarks I follow. I'm telling the client that once I'm satisfied with the methods and systems laid, and I see it being implemented religiously, and the results are to be seen, I know it's time for me to exit.

* *

During our pitch discussion, I mention that my appointment is your choice, but the exit is mine.

* *

In short, I will not leave till I don't give you results. I never burden the client or impose myself, but this working model is essential for clients to get that belief in me. I always put myself in my client's shoes and take the assignments forward. One way to do this is by complete hand-holding the client. It is easy to preach and tell what to do but biting the bullet myself is what I do. I get so deeply engrossed that my anchoring of all activities makes me an integral part.

Such involvement is crucial to not just impress the client, but I genuinely like to get underneath the skin of the problems. I also ensure clients are copied and posted on all actions we take. I always insist clients be present in review meetings to see how we are progressing, but this is not always possible and practical. We must capture the milestones, the short and small targets set, and celebrate success as we go along. The bigger picture matters the most, but one cannot underestimate small achievements.

* *

I always put myself in my client's shoes and take the assignments forward. One way to do this is by complete hand-holding the client.

* *

"A journey of a thousand miles begins with a single step" is a common saying from a Chinese proverb. This saying teaches that even the longest and most difficult ventures have a starting point, beginning with one first step.

* *

Questions to the reader:

1. Do you realize you require professional advice?

   ____

2. If yes, which are the areas you want to see results in?

   ____

3. What is the time frame you would be happy to see results coming in realistically?

   ____

4. Are you ready to allow someone like me to do a diagnostic study of your organization?

   ____

Which are the areas of my business you will be working on?

"Educating the mind without educating the heart is no education at all"

Aristotle

Primarily, I'm a generalist. Like you have a general practitioner in medicine, I'm a generalist in management & business practices.

This positioning of my generalist is crucial for my clients to understand how my business model works. While I'm experienced and have handled many clients in the past, what exactly and how do I get my deliverables to the table?

As mentioned earlier, my primary client profile is business owners from the MSME sector, and once their initial fire is extinguished, their bouncing boards, which they have in the form of their close relatives and friends, run dry of ideas, they need us.

****

This positioning of my generalist is crucial for my clients to understand how my business model works.

****

The initial meeting when I pitch or am called for is usually for a general overview. Slowly as comforts are established, some discussion happens on the commercials attached; then the client is keen to know - how I will address every problem of theirs. No one is perfect, informed or knowledgeable on all business functions, namely, HR, Finance, Accounts, Sales & Marketing, IT or Production & Operations. These are mainly the broad functions of any company, irrespective of its industry.

While I'm an Engineer and have an edge in the technical side of the business, my fondness and liking for sales & marketing made me improvise on this function. Besides these, I have created a panel of experts, a pool of extraordinary talent on my Board. I utilize the services of these very talented and knowledgeable people as and when the need arises. For e.g., we have IT experts who need domain knowledge of hardware and software, from sourcing the right, apt and established ERP systems and buying the proper hardware for the company to even exploring the new-age models which are nimble and economical for the company. I offer such domain expertise because of this strong team I have.

* *

I have created a panel of experts, a pool of extraordinary talent on my Board. I utilize the services of these very talented and knowledgeable people as and when the need arises.

* *

Interestingly, I offer and, as mentioned, do not impose myself on them to make me involved everywhere, but when we get an outside expert for a specific task, the client often insists on my presence and lead the way for them.

Questions to the reader:

1. Which department of yours lacks expertise?

   ----

2. Given the above position filled in what difference would it make to your current status of business?

How did I become a Trainer?

"Take all the training you can get; one good idea is all you need to save yourself years of hard work"

Brian Tracy

I'm an Engineer by qualification but was never attracted to the creation part of the industry. I like to engage and interact with people. As mentioned earlier, the trauma and challenges I've faced in my personal life helped me connect with the turmoil people go through in their lives. I discovered that I have that knack for identifying the pain points and then addressing them specifically. Over a period of time, with experience and practice, I could further improvise.

Two significant events in my life were instrumental in my journey of becoming a Trainer.

****

I discovered that I have that knack for identifying the pain points and then addressing them specifically. Over a period of time, with experience and practice, I could further improvise.

****

The first was because of the book by Stephen Covey; The 7 Habits of Highly Effective People, namely:

- Habit 1: Be Proactive®
- Habit 2: Begin With the End in Mind®
- Habit 3: Put First Things First®
- Habit 4: Think Win-Win®
- Habit 5: Seek First to Understand, Then to Be Understood®
- Habit 6: Synergize®
- Habit 7: Sharpen the Saw®

Even today, I'm mesmerized by this book. Every habit, quote and explanation has got stuck in my mind. I use this book in my training for reference, notes etc. and also explain how to put these into practice. In our current era of over-information supply with whatever you need to know, just a click away, these 7 Habits are on the search engines and can be found easily. What is crucial for the reader to know and get trained is to understand how to practice these and get astonishing results in their lives for effective transformation.

Besides the book content, which I touch upon, I focus on the "how to do it" aspect, how to put in practice what Stephen Covey has said.

In my training, I help to:

Write mission statements, comprising of:

- Writing a Tombstone Statement
- Drafting a Mission song
- How to find a role model
- Set core values
- Defining Roles & Goals

Primarily, I'm a Soft-Skill Trainer, and my areas of expertise include:

- Team-building
- Communication
- Paradigm
- Pro-activeness
- Time Management
- Role Management
- Delegation
- Synergistic working model

The second event which helped me believe that I'm made to become a Trainer was Landmark Worldwide.

Landmark Worldwide, or simply Landmark, is a company headquartered in San Francisco that offers personal-development programs. Landmark Education started in 1991 with the licensing of rights to use intellectual property owned by Werner Erhard, who had originated in the 1970s.

It aims to bring about positive, permanent shifts in the quality of your life. Create power, freedom, full self-expression, and peace of mind® for your future.

More than 94% of participants surveyed reported The Landmark Forum made a profound and lasting difference in their lives.

The Landmark Forum is designed to bring about positive, permanent shifts in the quality of your life–in just three days. These shifts are the direct cause for a new and unique kind of freedom and power–the freedom to be at ease and the power to be effective in the areas that matter most to you: the quality of your relationships, the confidence with which you live your life, your personal productivity, your experience of the difference you make, your enjoyment of life.

Please refer: www.landmarkworldwide.com

* *

More than 94% of participants surveyed reported The Landmark Forum made a profound and lasting difference in their lives.

* *

Having heard many success stories about Landmark, I enrolled on its course and must admit; it was a transformational event for me. I was highly charged and inspired by the speaker Ferdie D'Souza.

These two events made me take an interest in the Training profession.

I've seen the training industry evolve all these years. From the times of the OHP (Over Head Projector), the acetates, which at some point I must be owning over a thousand, the LCDs to the eventual Powerpoint presentations. I've seen the entire journey of how then a trainer used to go about to now, where technology plays a crucial role.

Zig Ziglar trained us on how to deliver the training material and also on our preparation. You must have seen trainers fumbling, unprepared for their presentations, searching for notes and references etc. We were taught right from the basics of:

- Know your room
- Understand the technology and systems present in the room

- Set your audience seating arrangements as you need
- Prepare your notes
- Storytelling
- Audio & Video clips
- Entertainment
- Engagement techniques
- Notes to handover

....and many more things like these to ensure the audience is glued to you. The ability to engage and ensure the audience stays with you is crucial to achieving effectiveness.

One practice I learned at Landmark was the Time Cards model. The Cards are an indication shown to the speaker if one is deviating, losing focus, spending too much time on a topic, getting into arguments etc. This is a masterstroke model to groom anyone.

I also realized that one of my most essential assets besides the content I deliver is my voice. Top singers and voiceover artists take care of their throats. As a trainer, I needed to take care of that as well. I started drinking warm water during the sessions, and my assistants were trained to accompany me with all the tools and gadgets I needed, including warm water. Such is my engagement during these sessions, the involvement and passion with which I work, is that I often get carried away, leave things behind like my blazer or jacket etc. I am fortunate to have assistants who know my requirements even before I realize I need them. They read my facial expressions or my curiosity in searching for something and hand it over before I can even look at them. My team has played a significant role in my success.

People attending training members look upon you as their saviour or demi-God and expect miracles. One has to live up to their expectations to the best of one's ability. This is possible by defining the goalposts clearly. They must be told precisely what they will get from these training sessions. Eventually, "What's In It For Me" is what everyone looks for. Unless we deliver something they do not know or have heard of, they will not find the sessions enjoyable.

I know that the best of the training can just vanish in thin air once the sessions are over. The more committed may retain their notes, go through them again and even implement a few things.

People are generally shy and do not talk in these training sessions. To make sure people carry the learnings forward and implement them, my team and I follow these practices:

- Breaking the audience into smaller groups.
- Encourage sharing.
- Giving feedback for small incremental or significant changes being experienced.
- Exercises to be completed.
- Provide adequate notes.
- Assistants are provided for further explanations and follow-up sessions.

* *

People attending training members look upon you as their saviour or demi-God and expect miracles. One has to live up to their expectations to the best of one's ability.

* *

I want to mention here an incident which happened many years back on something I had never expected. This can happen to any trainer.

A training session was scheduled for a Bank. The staff was sent with me to a resort to conduct a two-day programme. We were to start the session, and a group of people told me to stop what I was about to do those two days and enjoy the resort and then we all could happily go back home. I did not get into arguments, bring my ego to the forefront, or say that I would report this to the Board etc. I only requested the group to give me ninety minutes and listen to me. I told them to keep aside the Bank's need for this training and listen to me to help them change their lives, improve relationships, set goals, etc. I told them we would travel back home happily if this didn't work.

It worked because I had submitted, not confronted.

We trainers often find and spot the trouble-makers in the audience, and the ones who cannot do so in the first five minutes can get into trouble. The following helps:

- Knowing the audience and their profile in advance.
- The history of the sessions they have attended in the past.
- What kind of speakers have addressed them in the past?
- The groups in which they sit. Shifting the pattern and breaking the groups helps.
- The body language of certain people. The folded hands indicate defensiveness and "I know what you are saying" signals. One trick is getting them on your side by acknowledging their seniority and knowledge. Making them contribute to your deliverables boosts their ego, and suddenly, they feel a notch above all.

- Entertainment wrapped in your content with chocolate at the end as medicine works well. Do not impose yourself but say what you need to in their way.

- Storytelling is the best way to explain and highlight the takeaways rather than giving a list of things to do.

* *

We trainers often find and spot the trouble-makers in the audience, and the ones who cannot do so in the first five minutes can get into trouble.

* *

Question to the reader:

Do you like to attend training sessions?

____

What elements of the training sessions work the best for you from the following? How would you rate each of these on a scale of 10 (1 being the best)?

- Short-duration - 60-90 mins sessions.
- Audio & Video clips in between.
- Surprise guest speakers in between.
- Storytelling.
- Participation rather than a monologue.
- Like to receive notes.
- Want follow-up sessions.
- Happy to get an assistant for implementation.

Your name:

Profession & Designation:

Email id:

Take a picture of the ratings given and send me on apggmc@gmail.com.

There's a lucky draw with this activity. If you are one amongst the selected three, I will send you a Zoom link for a FREE thirty minutes orientation session on either of the topics:

- Goal Setting
- How to find your right mentor?
- Time management techniques

How did I become a Counsellor?

"Faith is unseen but felt, faith is strength when we feel we have none, faith is hope when all seems lost"

Catherine Pulsifer

Like most life events, counselling came to me, not by planning.

In my training sessions on Soft Skills and Kaizen, I used to address a group of people. I always emphasised the implementation aspect in my training, but it was not always possible to drill down the practices to every attendee. The participants used to meet me later and insisted on conducting one-on-one sessions with them to understand further what I taught in the open training sessions. That was how I got into counselling. As I established myself in the training industry, I added three counselling sessions, so that they are able to implement it in their real-life situations.

But how did I learn to counsel?

Counselling can be taught, and many institutes also run a course. Father Orlando Rodrigues at the Father Agnel Technical Complex at Vashi said to counsel; you should eradicate any distance between the counselee and yourself first. Maintaining eye contact and sound body language is equally crucial for the conversation to be effective. These are little gems I picked up during my association with him, which remained with me till date and I have been implementing them.

How did people confide in me, or why did they do so?

One specific reason I can gauge is the experience I bring to the table. I've seen it all. People around me, the clients, associates, friends, and vendors, all know what I have gone through and how I have emerged from the situations. This is one reason I think people confide in me. My counselees tell me that they like my counselling style because I hand-hold and allow them to express themselves. I do not enforce conditions and give them a choice on multiple options to try. Many times, they come with problems and also solutions. It is just that they need to get it authorised or want someone with whom they can reaffirm it. Since they are in a dilemma and surrounded by multiple challenges, talking to someone helps.

There are no magic formulas, a fixed pattern or a process to counsel. What works on one may not work on the other. The situations are different; the age group of counselees is diverse, and the language and skills I need to implement in each of these have to be different.

****

I have some interesting stories to share about my counselling engagements.

There was once a child who was considered retarded and who had become the core of the problem for a married couple. The husband almost abandoned his wife, and the family kept their distance from this lady and the child.

She came to me for counselling, and something told me that the situation was not as bad as it appeared. Maybe a change in the surrounding, company of people or a house could probably work, was my gut feeling. Coincidentally, the family's home went into re-development and they had to shift elsewhere. After meeting the child, the new school the child was enrolled in insisted that he needed to skip one year and start from Grade one instead of Grade two, where he was supposed to start. This worked like magic; the child could cope with the situation, was less stressed and gradually showed no signs of being retarded. The relationship between the family improved. The husband and wife bonded well and had another child.

****

In another case, a man approached me with a marital affair. His wife came to know about this, and this man was under stress to handle the situation. I advised him to leave the new lady in his life and live happily with his wife, and he listened to this. The complication started when the other lady threatened him with dire consequences if he walked off from her life. The man was in a complete fix and approached me again for the advice. I had to tell him not to bother about the consequences and look at the problems in the eyes. Face the issue rather than running away. I told him to say to the lady to do whatever she wished, for which he was not ready. Eventually, I had to advise him to step on both the stones and live happily, managing both the ladies but taking adequate care. While he continues to have this affair, he is also keeping his wife happy.

****

A man had a child who refused to go to school, and the family was not finding the answers to convince him. They had tried everything, but nothing worked. The family came to me for advice.

I met the child and offered him help by telling him that if anyone forced him to go to school, he could call me. I gave my visiting card to him and said he could call me anytime if anyone tried to influence him. Now, I was by his side, and for once, he must have felt that there was someone who was with him. Many days passed, and the family became anxious. They were worried as a fortnight had passed and he was missing school. They called me, and I assured them to trust me with what I was doing. One day, the child saw his mother ironing the uniform for his elder brother, who used to go to the same school. He went to his mother and said he would also want to go to school and she should prepare him. When asked why his mind changed, he said he felt left out. He sensed his friends were talking about something he couldn't connect on every evening. He had nothing to do the whole day as all his friends went to school. This was enough for him to change his view.

****

All this tells me that my microscopic and telescopic approach works well in assessing situations. I have no set formulas or patterns of counselling. There's no fixed process. When I take a view from the top, it appears different, and when I get to the root of the issue, it's a different perspective. I'm dispassionate and try to look for something not seen or told by the person coming to me for counselling. There's a story behind every story, which is what must be unfolded.

How did I become a Consultant?

"A Consultant to be worth his salt must give honest judgments not necessarily those which he thinks the clients would like to hear"

Andrew Thomas

My logical progress should have been in the same field because of my qualification as an Engineer. But, one never knows how things take a turn.

Typically, as a youngster would think, I wanted to try many things and got into an exploratory mode. I opted to become a Project Management Consultant and tasted success, too, but I realised one thing it was becoming a commoditised business. There were too many limitations in this field as the scope was not to add value but to manage the proceedings. I soon realised not only would I make less money but also not contribute significantly to show my real potential only on improvements in labour issues, buying raw materials efficiently etc.

Most importantly, I was not getting that satisfaction in my work.

What always excited me was dealing with people, solving their challenges, addressing them unbiasedly, delivering results, and hand-hold them in execution. I had to broaden my canvas and I did.

I saw there's tremendous scope in offering consultancy to the MSME sector. The companies here needed a holistic consultancy - someone who can offer all aspects from HR, Finance & Accounts, Marketing & Sales, IT, and Operations to Administrative functions to manage their company and progress towards growth. While I am not an expert in all these fields, I developed the skills. My course at the IIM Ahmedabad to learn about the MSME helped me gain deep insight. HR was always my strength as I was influenced by and followed the great Stephen Covey. Operations came to me because I learned Kaizen, best manufacturing practices, etc. Being an entrepreneur myself, I had to learn Accounts and also Finance. Teaching Finance to non-finance executives was something I focused on.

Unfortunately, for the MSMEs, their Chartered Accountant (CA) is their primary advisory source, and most of the time, their discussions revolve around saving tax. Chartered Accountants are historians as they come into the picture when numbers are ready. Nothing wrong with that, as that's their line of work, but what needs to be done earlier is where I come in. Reading a balance sheet and analysing data became my strength too. I took a keen interest in all these. Marketing & Sales came to me quickly as I was trained with my initial exposure in the Insurance industry. The insurance companies' training is outstanding to groom anyone who wishes to make it big in sales. Another organisation, BNI (Business Network International), helped me to further polish my sales skills. If done consistently, the training and activities are of international standards and can take one to the next level in networking, sales, and relationship building. The learnings are life-long and help you become a Networker of international class. I'm currently still a BNI member and contribute to it. It also teaches how to conduct meetings, manage people of different backgrounds, follow laid policies, etc. All this contributes to your personal growth. I was fortunate to launch a new chapter and perform various roles, from leading the chapter as the President and as a Lead Visitor Host to anchoring Educational slots for the chapter.

****

What always excited me was dealing with people, solving their challenges, addressing them unbiasedly, delivering results, and hand-hold them in execution. I had to broaden my canvas, and I did.

****

The journey is still on, and every passing day helps me become a better professional, contributing to my capacity as a Trainer, Counsellor, and Consultant.

How do I perform my duty as a Consultant?

I usually start with a FREE session. Many advised me and even insisted on charging some fee for this first session, but ever since I started my business, I've never charged for this first session. For me, it is crucial to assess the situation first.

I get into a diagnostic mode and evaluate the damage, need, and solutions most needed. This activity of analysing and recommending has come after years of practice, the ability to map and plot against similar situations, and deep insight to know where the real problem lies. If the assignment doesn't suit me or I think I cannot justify it, I very honestly decline the offer myself but not before guiding the client to the best-suited person.

If I come on board, I have an Executive Assistant with me who is deeply involved in Company matters. From taking notes, and drafting minutes to ensuring the action points are acted upon from the owner to the staff member involved; he anchors the execution. When all activities are done, he reports back to me, and we move on to the next session and repeat likewise.

* *

This activity of analysing and recommending has come after years of practice, the ability to map and plot against similar situations, and deep insight to know where the real problem lies.

* *

As mentioned earlier, when I'm fully convinced that my role is done and the client is now able to run the show well, I quit. I decide when to leave; I know when the time is up. Such honesty, integrity, and transparency are what clients appreciate. While on average, my engagement with a client for consultancy is from one to three years, even after quitting, many clients have called me back as their businesses evolve with changing times. New challenges and new goalposts emerge, and that is where they need me again. Such is the immense satisfaction I get in my role that I'm blessed to have come into this profession where I'm truly contributing to people's growth.

****

Here are a few case studies in my role as a Consultant:

My first significant assignment occurred when I was in association at Father Agnel Technical Complex. In 1996, I was introduced to M/s. P.D. Construction, who was given the task to build a factory for their client Amrut Doodh. The task was challenging as failure to complete the construction within one year would result in a penalty of five lacs rupees, and the bonus was also of the equivalent amount if the task was done within a year. This amount was big way back in the mid-nineties when I was on board as their Project Management Consultant but we could complete the project earning a five lacs bonus for my client. The owner, Dilipbhai Shah, was so happy that he also asked me to mentor his son Vipul Shah in his career.

I think what worked well was adjusting to the new cultural change India was getting into. Incentives for good work and penalties for a bad job were relatively new then. I remember, in the late nineties, even the Indian cricketers were offered incentives if they held on to catches or scored a fifty or a century. This culture was exciting, and Dilipbhai accepted the challenge. All it took me was to drive the process correctly, as the will was already in place.

As explained earlier, the MSME sector needs a generalist as their consultant, and as they progress and reach a threshold, their challenges mature. The need for a specialist comes later. As a consultant for an Electrical panel builder, I got this opportunity when I was associated with the LAKSHYAVEDH Institute of Leadership & Excellence in the role of a mentor for many. I could hand-hold them in their growth, and when they reached the threshold of a turnover of five crores, they called me again to help them achieve their next turnover goal. It is a very technical industry, and with new technologies from AI to Robotics, their challenges to adapt to new practices will only grow. The client had to look professionally at the industry and the customer's unmet needs. We could streamline several activities from Marketing, Sales, and Finance to Customer service, which gave the company the right impetus to progress. We had to get into several practices never done by this company earlier. There was resistance, frustration and lack of participation initially, but finally, as everyone started seeing results, it worked. Here again, it was a cultural change that people had to adjust to, leading to our success.

I'm also happy to mention SangitaaRijhwani, Director, Rijhwaani Associates LLP. My association goes back more than two decades back with them. Theirs is a mutual fund and financial planning industry but my deep involvement with them, and the mentoring I could do with Late Shri

Manoj Rijhwaani and Sangitaaji brought me very close to their business. I helped them in their initial journey of building their business, mentored them professionally and built a company that runs on auto-pilot mode today.

The life insurance industry always fascinates me. Only 3.30% of India's population is covered under a life insurance plan, which gives us an idea of the scope of the potential. The Mutual Fund industry back then in the nineties was new, and there was already excitement to learn the new concepts. India was under the liberalisation and opening of the economy stage, and there was bullishness. New policies were planned, the Union Budgets was one big event all were glued to, and a lot was happening in the BFSI sector (Banking, Financial Services and Insurance). All this contributed to the sales training required for financial planners and agents with new products being launched frequently. I have always enjoyed working in this sector, and my passion probably also rubbed to the Rijhwaanis.

There was a time when I wanted to work with top management consultancy firms like E&Y, but then came a time when I was interviewing Executives from E&Y for my client who wanted to appoint them. Once I realised that the canvas had grown beyond me and I could not service my client's requirements, I always advised them to look for someone more competent than me. One such occasion was when the client wanted to buy a cricket team after becoming a five hundred crore organisation. I didn't have the capacity or the knowledge to handle this assignment. I recommended my client to appoint E&Y but my client insisted I do the interviewing and appointment.

The reader will relate to the mix of industries I have mentioned above. When the foundation is solidly established with best practices and international standards, when the intent is pure and honest, all it needs is to be deeply involved in delivering results in the client's best interest, which I am doing consistently.

HR practices

"Nothing we do is more important than hiring people. At the end of the day, you bet on people, not strategies"

Lawerence Bossidy

There are no bad employees; there are bad managers. There are no bad managers; there are bad owners/directors.

3M – HR policies

- We treat our employees the way they should treat the best customers.

- Once upon a time in India, there used to be Industrial Relationship Managers. The social changes of the 1960s & 1970s created a need for the “personnel” department to evolve into human resources.

- Embracing empathy, focusing on data and enabling analysis to drive strategy are three modern HR practices that today’s leading organizations deploy.
- The new trend is replacing the HR department with the people operation department.
- The challenges with MSME Entrepreneurs are many in the Human Resources department. Attitude toward employees generates out of their belief system that can be broadly divided into two.

Attracting better talent to business is one of the fore most responsibilities and, priorities of the HR dept. Similarly, reducing attrition on the one hand and cost on the other is the second challenge they face. The third one is up skilling workers & staff to improve productivity. On the other hand, employees face the challenge of work-life balance, stress at times and purposelessness. Day by day, a high level of job loss is becoming a way of life. This is inducing a lot of stress in the employees, and their morale is going down daily. Employee’s health has also taken a plunge.

Aspect	**Modern approach**	**Traditional /MSME approach**
Attitude	**Assets**	**Inevitable Evil**
Money spent	It's an investment.	It's a cost. Unavoidable liability
Profitable	We make more money if we have the right employees.	We make money in spite of employees.
Company	Good- Great	Company - Functioned
Treatment	Respect, trust	Contempt, neglect, de-test, despise, they are put Down
The important thing when you re-hire	All employees are not assets but the right employees are assets and getting them is a challenge.	

The issue of training and retraining employees is also highly relevant. Businesses need to understand the importance of employee training. The common complaints about employee training are:

1. It takes needed employees away from production activities, affecting productivity.

2. Employees use it as an opportunity to take a break from work and consider it as a leisure activity.

3. After employees return from training, they do not perform their job any better.

4. It is a drain on resources that produces no tangible results.

This problem arises because employee training is poorly administered and executed. Employee training should fill the gap in knowledge, skills, or attitudes of the individual whose work performance is suffering from those gaps. However, many organisations fail to identify the knowledge, & attitudes skill gaps of employees. Instead, employees are sent to training for:

1. Filling training quotas

2. As part of tradition or ritual rather than a need

3. As a disciplinary measure

4. To satisfy an employee's request

My personal experience of working with MSMEs is as follows:

Though we call them entrepreneurs, most of the SMEs are not entrepreneurs but they are just self-employed people. Most of them come into the business because of fire in their belly and a lot of common sense, which most people don't use. These owners are the last benchers in the classroom and do not have any respect for education. In most companies, being educated is a curse but having field experience is very important. Most of them need to understand that education & experience are two wheels of the same cart. They complement each other, and are notin conflict.

Because of the above attitude, training is not considered an essential aspect of the employees' performance development and, as a result, of the company's performance. Because of this understanding of the theoretical aspect, most owners are reluctant to engage consultants who generally come from backgrounds of both experience & qualification.

There is a general feeling amongst entrepreneurs that since they have been running their business for so many years, how can an outsider in the role of a consultant know better about their company than they do? What they need to understand is that any business needs to be looked at from a microscopic view as narrow as an ant and like a bird from a telescopic sight as well. Since business owners are so much involved in their operations, they cannot justify telescopic (long-term) involvement. It is impossible to balance both these aspects, so the need for additional professional help is essential.

Initially, when he starts a business, he is the peon, salesperson, production guy, accounts & finance guy, and so on & so forth. In a small business, the people around the owner may have the competence to suggest things that may work. They also work as bouncing boards. The owner can remember all the figures as if they are at his fingertips regarding sales, receivables, bank balances, etc. However, this support system does not deliver the goods as the business grows. In addition, the company crosses certain thresholds, due to which he now has to scrap the old methods that have brought in success & adopt new ways of doing business which he doesn't know. For example, initially, he may be able to remember all the numbers in the company up to the second digit, but as the business grows, his memory starts failing. His common sense can bring business to a certain level. Still, after that threshold, the company will require specific scientific inputs like statistics, sales marketing, human resource management, finance management, etc., to augment the additional know-how. The threshold in the business may be 25 lakhs,50 lakhs, 75 lakhs, 1 crore, 10 crores, 50 crores, 100 crores, and so on. One has to scrap old methods and adopt new techniques at each threshold. This challenge of constant change is highly stressful, and as a result, owners deny these challenges maintaining the ostrich mentality. (The ostrich effect, also known as the ostrich problem, is a cognitive bias that describes how people often avoid negative information, including feedback that could help them monitor their goal progress. Instead, if dealing with the situation, we bury our heads in the sand, like ostriches.)

My purpose which drives me all these years

"This is the true joy in life-that being used for a purpose recognized by yourself as a mighty one. That being a force of nature, instead of a feverish, selfish little clod of ailments and grievances complaining that the world will not devote itself to making you happy. I am of the opinion that my life belongs to the whole community and as long as I live it is my privilege to do for it whatever I can. I want to be thoroughly used up when I die. For the harder, I work the more I live. I rejoice in life for its own sake. Life is no brief candle to me. It's a sort of splendid torch which I've got to hold up for the moment and I want to make it burn as brightly as possible before handing it on to future generations."

George Bernard Shaw

Deep down in my heart, I'm a teacher, and I'm glad I realized it very early when I stepped into my eventual profession of being a consultant, trainer and counsellor to many. This is what drives me even today.

Such is the passion, commitment and engagement that I often forget to eat and drink. The degree of my involvement is a pleasure as I do not experience any pressure. When I retrospect, I realize I enjoy teaching and can go to any extent in transforming lives if there are ears to listen to me. Most importantly, the implementation has to be in place with utmost faith and belief in the process I lay, which is not short-term but long-term, with assured results. Obviously, both my realization of teaching and the results I could deliver did not happen overnight. But as much as I enjoyed the journey, the re-inventing of my processes, skill upgradation and adapting to changing needs is also something I keep an eye on. Businesses are changing more rapidly than ever; technology is evolving every minute, breakthroughs are a routine now, consumer behaviour is changing briskly, especially after the pandemic of coronavirus and the need for being nimble and de-risking your businesses has increased than earlier times. Strategies were once discussed once a year at a good resort and were a five-day affair; today, there is a review meeting for course correction every month or every week.

****

When I retrospect, I realize I enjoy teaching and can go to any extent in transforming lives if there are ears to listen to me.

****

The MSME sector is no different and needs a similar amount of effort and realization. They also need to grow and transform themselves into enterprises of having a large scale and even go global eventually. This is where I step in again to hand-hold these companies in their journey.

Over the years, I have realized a consistent pattern of behaviour. The first is people's resistance to sitting in my training and consultation to listen to me, leave alone implementation. My sessions are addressed to adults who develop this trait of non-acceptance and "I know everything" attitude and "what will he teach me". Another common observation is the body language of the people I observe. A person with folded arms across his chest indicates an unconscious attempt to block what one perceives as a threat. It is a classic gesture of defensiveness. Making them open up with free hands to express, and react is the primary task to start the ball rolling.

The second aspect I realized very early is unless I do not add an element of entertainment and storytelling in my sessions, I will not be able to grab their attention and ensure the teaching is registered in their mind. It is an achievement if I can confirm the message has seeped into them. What matters later are the follow-up sessions. The hook is essential to get going, or else I've seen expressions of people who are only present with their body in these sessions as the mind is already somewhere else.

Here's one story from one of the most successful assignments I've anchored:

The client: Corient Business Solutions
Corient supports Accountants and Businesses by providing Accounting, Payroll, Consulting, Back Office, Analytics, and Management Information services by blending the best of both- People and Technology.

Corient stands for Client (C) Oriented Company. All the things they do is undertaken with their Clients at the centre of it. They blend their services with state-of-the-art processes (best in class) with the client's company culture to provide tailor-made services to meet their requirements and help them focus on their core business.

My task was to grow the Company by 10X in the top and bottom line.

I met Mr Sachin Lohade, CEO & Founder of Corient, at the LAKSHYAVEDH Institute of Leadership & Excellence when he was felicitated as the best CEO. We could connect easily, and our conversation revolved around the books "Good to Great" and "Built To Last" by Jim Collins. These books are true masterpieces for any growing organization with its key concepts:

1. Level five leadership.
2. First who...then what.
3. Confront the brutal facts but don't lose faith.
4. The Hedgehog Concept.
5. A culture of discipline.

6. Technology – the accelerators

7. The flywheel and the doom loop.

8. From good to great to built to last.

I remember distinctly when Sachin said:

“how would we implement these concepts in our organization”.

At this juncture, he decided to get me on board to help him practice these concepts for his Company. He appointed me as their mentor, and the journey began.

I could get simplicity in the implementation process, which worked the best. These concepts are complicated and often require ruthless decisions, but Sachin and his team could absorb what I was trying to get to, achieving the desired success. We all get great wisdom from management books but often struggle to implement those. My style of teaching and execution is what worked at Corient and our association grew all these years.

Another area I could help Sachin was when he was facing

a personal dilemma. His inclination to the spiritual side, which conveys living within your means, essentialism and minimalism, conflicted with his Company's objectives of growth and profits. I could explain the philosophy of Trusteeship of Mahatma Gandhi, who said Trusteeship is a socio-economic philosophy - **It provides a means by which wealthy people become trustees of their businesses looking after the welfare of people in general.**

This profoundly impacted him, and Sachin could find the purpose. To further give this a direction, I recommended him contribute more towards society in general and also for the cause of animal welfare, planting trees, watering them regularly, etc. Several such initiatives were started, which helped him find the right balance.

Entrepreneurs often face these challenges. While putting your core values and beliefs are important to drive the organization, how you actually practices equally matters.

When I was appointed with Corient, the people's strength was 150; today, it is close to 450. While the brief was clear to me, I knew at first assessment that the problem was at the top of the pyramid. The bottleneck is always at the top of the bottle.

Only having a will, a strong desire or an aspiration doesn't help. One has to bite the bullet, take tough decisions, be ready to accept challenges by looking into its eyes and not shy away but most importantly, be prepared to transform in mind first. Telling yourself repeatedly and visualising a picture of growth or where you want to see your company was needed. If you think small, you will remain small. If you think big, expand your horizons, broaden the canvas and stretch your imagination, it starts working. The power of manifestation leading to the desired transformation cannot be underestimated. It begins with your faith in the picture you want to see. This ability to manifest was something I had to first imbibe in the Promoters and top-level Executives at Corient. Half the battle was won here when this was accepted and implemented.

****

We all get great wisdom from management books but often struggle to implement those. My style of teaching and execution is what worked at Corient and our association grew all these years.

****

Then came the company assessment, which I did in-depth, and I had to tell them that I would get into the minutest of details in every department. As expected, there was a tremendous amount of resistance, but eventually, everyone started seeing results. Culture is bigger than strategy, which has to come in line before you can get the desired contribution from your people. It was not easy as I had to introduce new processes and systems and even change people, which was the toughest of the tasks, but it was all in the company's interest.

****

Telling yourself repeatedly and visualising a picture of growth or where you want to see your company was needed. If you think small, you will remain small. If you think big, expand your horizons, broaden the canvas and stretch your imagination, it starts working there.

****

A few things I had to put my foot down were in the areas of

Human Resources, which is the closest to me. Selecting the right people in sales, grooming & training them, correcting their sales pitch, targeting the right markets and giving broader strategies in marketing where required. My role was to drive this change as the promoters were capable of execution. All they needed was that push from my side. We revisited the marketing strategies and the new avenues available to get the right leads and then focused on converting these leads. From Google Ads, social media, and digital marketing to SEO, no stone was left unturned. All the energy went into areas where things were working, pushing it further and eliminating the ones that were not fetching results.

Finally, we could achieve a 7.5X growth which was more than double their average yearly growth rate. Today, the company is on course to scale further, and I'm still on board to help them drive further. I may not be an expert in all the areas, but Corient could read my ability to drive and anchor their activities, assess in an unbiased manner and keep shifting the strategies to achieve as per new goal posts they are setting for themselves.

****

Culture is bigger than strategy, which has to come in line before you can get the desired contribution from your people.

****

Questions to the reader:

1. Have you tried defining your purpose?

   ____

2. What is your purpose in life (personal and professional)?

   ____

   ____

What do I stand for?

"Keep your thoughts positive as your thoughts become your words. Keep your words positive because your words become your behaviour. Keep your behaviour positive as your behaviour becomes your habit. Keep your habits positive as your habits become your values. Keep your values positive as your values become your destiny."

Mahatma Gandhi

We often say, "he or she is a person of great substance". Every person stands for something. What is the image you carry? What is it that you are known for to the outside world? What statement do you make when you enter a room?

Your values define all this; even if you don't intentionally practice this, people notice it. The people outside will always say and recognize this quickly. Right from our childhood, parents see it. Remember you were called a "*badmaash*" - this term for a parent is not to say in its negative meaning but to mean how clever we are, how uncompromising we are (hard-working), how stubborn we are (determined), how we don't give up (relentless taskmaster) and will find our way in anyhow, we are innocent, etc. It all starts there.

As we grow, we start realizing what we stand for, and so did I. It came naturally to me what I cannot tolerate and what I will practice no matter what.

Here are a few core values I have practised all these years. I obviously practice what I preach. I help companies form their tombstone statements, their mission and vision statements and identify core values; how would I not have those for myself?

Here are my core values:

- Integrity: Match external and internal being

- Dignity: All beings have the right to self-respect

- Equality: All beings are born equal

- Passion: Anything I do, do it passionately

- Scientific Approach: Lighthouse principal
- Contribution: I enjoy being a contributor to a situation/life
- Kaizen: No matter what, everything can be improved continuously
- Commitment: A promise is a promise no matter what
- Student for life.

Let me elaborate on a few for the readers.

Passion:

The degree of my involvement and engagement with the tasks I take at hand can go to any level. I know the ill effects, but I cannot stop myself when it comes to my work. I don't sleep, eat or look at my watch when there are tasks at hand. I leave no stone unturned.

In one such counselling assignment, a young girl came to me with her personal challenges and, over time, got so involved with me that it went beyond professional engagement. I had to end that and explain to the girl of my daughter's age that this was a professional engagement and I was here only to help her give her that right direction and nothing beyond that.

Fortunately, everything ended well, and she is happily living with her family today.

The extent to which my involvement takes me results from my passion for my work. No matter what you do, it would be best to immerse yourself in meeting the desired objectives.

Dignity:

This value helps you look into the mirror with grace. Can you be a part of something which you do not believe in? Of course not.

There was once a client who got me on Board for consulting. On the first day itself, in front of me, he was yelling at staff and abusing them for some reason. I could not take that, and I walked out. Later, he asked me what made me walk out, to which I explained how he dealt with that employee was wrong, especially in front of me. It appeared that I was also a part of that since I was not saying anything, which hurt me the most. I told him I would handle these situations if he's brought me in. There's a way of handling things, and every person's dignity needs to be taken care of.

Here was a case where I was ready to walk out no matter what money the client was prepared to pay me. In life, you have to stick to your core values, and I was happy I got this opportunity to put in place what I believe in.

Lighthouse principal:

A lighthouse helps you navigate the maritime world. It is the direction which matters. In life, we have penal laws, and there are spiritual laws. Violating penal laws lead to monetary losses or imprisonment, but deviating from your spiritual rules will make you guilty for the rest of your life, even if no one knows what you have done. Your inner voice will not allow you to rest or lead a peaceful life. To follow or adhere to spiritual laws, you need to run marathons of life and not just sprints.

Contribution:

This value also comes from passion. If I cannot deliver meaningfully, I will walk out or even may not accept the assignment in the first place. I'm ruthless to myself and set very high standards of performance and delivery. I have to make a difference in the life I'm touching to have that lasting impact. My footprints will be there to be seen even when I'm not with the person or the organization. This value helps me sleep well every night as I know I'm giving my best and making a difference to someone.

Commitment:

This core value is your face. Do you appear committed? Do you behave and give that message to anyone depicting commitment? Do people get that confidence when they give you a task to complete and when you assure them it will be done? What is your commitment to failure ratio? People associate commitment with reliability also. Are you reliable?

Further, reliability leads to trust. There is a thin line separating commitment, reliability and trust - each having its importance and these are built in stages. You get every opportunity to prove yourself; you must grab it as your commitment depicts who you are.

Here's a story of two brothers sent to the battlefield during the Second World War in Germany as the country's call demanded it. It was a fierce battlefield, and the brothers fought courageously. The enemy was advancing from all sides, and their Captain ordered them to retreat and return to their previous positions. There was chaos and confusion, and in this the brothers got separated. The elder brother realized that, the younger one was not around and asked his Captain to allow him to return and find his brother. The Captain was not in favour as there was danger as the enemy was firing. The Captain was furious and even mentioned to the elder brother that denying his orders could lead to him being court-martialled. The elder brother couldn't stop as he had to return for his brother. He finally found his younger one lying in a pool of blood with injuries. He lifted him on his shoulder, but the young one looked at him and said, "I knew you would come for me, and I was alive only to see you", and then he died.

This story tells the belief the younger one had in his elder brother for the commitment he carried. I often narrate this story in my sessions to explain the power and belief of commitment. Once someone believes in you - no matter what, they know you will deliver. This is an image you need to build and deliver consistently.

* *

We often say, "he or she is a person of great substance". Every person stands for something. What is the image you carry? What is it that you are known for to the outside world? What statement do you make when you enter a room?

* *

Question to the reader:

1. What do you stand for?

   ____

The art of storytelling

"Nothing sticks in your head better than a story. Stories can explain the most complex ideas in the most digestible ways"

Sam Balter

In the world of Sales, there's a saying–"Facts tell, but stories sell".

The meaning behind this saying is obvious. **If you want a person to purchase your products or services, you must tell them a story**. It is not just in Sales. Apply this to any function, and you can put forward your view or idea effectively.

The MSME sector I primarily deal with requires storytelling more than anyone. The owners, most of the time, are back-benchers and street-smart. They often hire the ones who sit on the front benches in school. These owners of the MSMEs need solutions which work instantly. They want to see and hear something that explains them easily without jargon or heavy management words.

Storytelling is the answer to it.

Now, look at this. I had to explain the importance of promotion, awareness and visibility, for which I use this favourite story in my sessions.

Why does a hen's egg sell more?

A duck and a hen both lay eggs. Size-wise, the duck's egg is much larger than a hen's egg. Both are equally nutritious. However, why are hen's eggs more popular than the ducks? Why do people eat more hen's eggs?

If you closely observe the laying process of an egg by a duck and hen, you will get the answer. When the duck lays the egg very silently, she will look left, right and lay the egg, and move away. If you observe a hen laying an egg, you will find the hen at the top of her voice announcing that she has laid an egg.....Cock Cock Cock Cock!!

Learning from this story: It is essential to advertise your product to the people for them to buy.

Note – Actually, the egg of a duck, though it carries all the qualities, has a particular smell because of which people do not prefer that egg. However, this story is to educate our entrepreneurs about the importance of visibility & communication of their products and services, which is essential.

****

I'm often asked during my counselling sessions how to follow "punya" and "paap".

The Nyaya School understands dharma and adharma to refer to punya and paap, with **punya relating to one's own or others' well-being and paap relating to harm done to others, or in terms of doing one's duties and their violation;** it connects dharma to well-being and duty.

(https://en.wikipedia.org/wiki/Punya_(Hinduism)#:~:text=The%20Ny%C4%81ya%20School%20understands%20dharma,to%20well%2Dbeing%20and%20duty.)

I narrate a story to explain “punya” and “paap”.

A girl once was chased by a group of people and met a person in the middle of nowhere. She begs to be protected from the people chasing her, and this person tells her to hide behind him in some corner where she cannot be seen. The group approaches this person and asks for the girl, to which he points in the wrong direction to misguide them. In this context, he lied or committed a “paap”, as lying is considered an incorrect value one doesn’t practice, but in the interest of protecting the girl’s life, he lied and thus, it cannot be considered a “paap”. Saving a life is of top priority.

The point is to note that sometimes a larger interest and objective needs to be protected. Life-saving is a higher value one should practice.

****

We sometimes commit wrongdoings or even know our actions or decisions are wrong. Still, because we delay coming out of the situation, our misery continues, and we, unfortunately, build that image which is tough to shed.

In the epic Mahabharata, Lord Krishna made that last attempt one night before the war between the Pandavas and Kauravas, requesting Duryodhana not to go to war. Duryodhana heard Lord Krishna and admitted knowing he was committing adharma and that he could not give up at that stage even though he knew the consequences of the forthcoming loss of lives and disaster in the making. He politely asks Lord Krishna to return back.

Duryodhana said, I know dharma but I have travelled on the path of adharma so long that now even if I wish I will not be able to follow dharma. (*Janami dharmam na cha me pravrutthih, janami adharmam na cha me nivrutthih. Translation: This verse is from the Mahabharata where Duryodhana says to Krishna: I know what is dharma (good conduct), yet I don't have the inclination for it. I know what is adharma, yet I cannot leave it)*.

Imagine what would have happened had Duryodhana listened to Lord Krishna.

As leaders, we need to learn from this and be adaptive and responsible to correct our wrongdoings.

****

Once there was an Arab who was riding on a camel in the desert. Though the days are hot in the desert, the Arabs prefer to ride the whole day to rest at night. But the nights can be extremely cold too. Out of no choice but to build their energy for the next day, they relax, and so do the camels. On one such night, when the Arab was resting, he saw the camel peeping into the tent, requesting the Arab to accommodate his head in the tent as it was freezing outside, which the Arab allowed. After sometime, the Arab saw that the camel had put his neck inside the tent, to which he objected but was considerate. The camel subsequently requested his body to be allowed in, and slowly the entire camel was inside the tent. The Arab had no choice but to walk out, and he found himself stranded and standing outside the tent in the cold.

If you allow people to take you for granted, they can take undue advantage. When systems are correctly set to run the business, and the processes are in place, the expectations become more precise, and your people also understand their boundaries.

****

My recommended Books to read& why?

"There are many little ways to enlarge your world. Love of books is the best of all"

Jacqueline Kennedy

Here is a list of books I strongly recommend my readers to read. These books are nothing short of an inspiration, motivation, and knowledge bank. I often refer to them and every time I glance through, there's something new I learn.

- **7 Habits of Highly Effective People" by Stephen Covey**

This book is a 7course meal for developing your emotional quotient & every person working in the business or even with NGO's, or Government agencies must read & implement the teachings of this book. This is not a novel to be read casually, but it's a reference manual for implementation & accessing a great life.

- **Built to Last and Good To Great by Jim Collins**

These books are like the Bible or Quran or Bhagavad-Gita for anybody in business, especially for the entrepreneurs to build their organisation which will last for centuries and become from a good company to a great company.

- **I'm Ok - You're OK by Thomas A. Harris M.D**

This is a book on transactional analysis. Every person has three characters: a child, a parent and an adult. When interacting with others, it is essential to know if my child, adult or parent is interacting with another person's child, adult or parent. Child-to-child or child-to-parent is an effective relationship, and communication and adult to adult is effective & productive communication. Adult-to-child or Adult to parent does not work and creates disaster, and we usually do not understand why it is so; this results in a feeling of I'm not ok, and you are not ok, because of which we suffer throughout our life. If we want to overcome suffering and enjoy our life, this book is a practical document for learning and implementation.

- **7 Habits Of Highly Effective Teens by Sean Covey**

This is a book written by Dr. Stephen Covey's son Sean Covey. This is a must-read for not only teenagers but their parents as well. After going through this book, a teenager will enjoy the wonderment of being a teen and can confidently deal with the challenges of his situation arising through miss communication, peer pressure, heartbreaks, love affairs, smoking, drugs and so on & so forth. The book will also guide parents in dealing with their teenage children.

- **World Of Kaizen by ShyamTalawadekar**

Kaizen means continuous improvement. The Kaizen philosophy is based on the fact that our life, whether working or social or family or between friends, needs constant improvement. If one is in the manufacturing or service industry, I am sure he is concerned with quality. Kaizen is an answer for all those issues arising from the production process or services you provide. In the case of the Toyota revolution, Kaizen laid the foundation for such a revolution.

- **The World Is Flat by Thomas L. Friedman**

This book is a brief history of the 21st century analysing globalisation. The title is a metaphor for viewing the world as a level playing field in terms of commerce where all competitors except for labour have an equal opportunity. The book also provides a perceptual shift required for countries, companies and individuals to remain competitive in the global market in which historical and geographic divisions are becoming irrelevant.

- **The Man Who Sold His Ferrari by Robin Sharma**

This is a self-help book written by Robin Sharma, a motivational speaker. The book is a business fable derived from Sharma's personal experience after leaving his career as a litigation lawyer at the age of 25. This book develops around two characters Julian Mantle & his best friend John, in the form of conversation. Julian narrates his spiritual experience during a Himalayan journey, which he undertook after selling his holiday home and Ferrari. Julian finally studied the seven virtues of the sages of Sivana in the Himalayan mountain. The book teaches you how to build a life that guarantees long-lasting happiness and fulfilment. It enlightens you that focusing on building your inner life is more important than making your outer life.

- **Build From Scratch by Vineet Bajpai**

With just fourteen thousand rupees, Vineet Bajpai formed one of the country's largest digital media company & became a self-propelled neo-tycoon. This book is a powerful guide for inspiring entrepreneurs through various tactics and steps of building an organisation from an idea. The book discusses critical topics of idea generation, fundraising, venture capital, go-to-market strategies and leadership. It also explores the human aspect of being an entrepreneur - the struggle, the ambition & the perseverance. It has a gritty & street-smart flavour that offers the most realistic and down-to-earth strategies. If you do not hail from a business family, you are not a Harvard dropout & you do not even have a world-changing innovation... & yet you dream of building your own company one day, build from scratch will be your soulmate.

- **Who Moved My Cheese? by Dr. Spencer Johnson**

The book is an amazing way to deal with changes in your work and life. It is a metaphor for what we want in life (a job, power status, relationships). The maize is a metaphor for which you spend your time looking for what you want (within the organisation, outside it, in the community, at home, etc.) It illustrates the importance of being able to deal with unexpected change. However, in such a relatable manner, you can read it in one sitting and walk away with a wealth of knowledge that will forever alter how you live your life.

* *

All books mentioned herein can be purchased from leading e-commerce platforms and bookstores globally as available

* *

Question to the reader:

1. Which are the books you have read (your Top 5 or 10)?

    ____

    ____

    ____

    ____

    ____

Leadership & Culture

"A true leader has the confidence to stand alone, the courage to make tough decisions and the compassion to listen to the needs of others. He does not set out to be a leader but becomes one by the equality of his actions and the integrity of his intent."

Douglas MacArthur

I deliberately chose the topics of leadership and culture to be written last in my book. I want the readers to remember this chapter the most, for this will be the most vital point of your business.

Leaders are born, but they can also be made. As an entrepreneur, you may have a great model of doing business, a great product or service, but you must lead your team from a long-term point of view to avoid hitting a wall. In times of adversity, your people will have to stand by you, and for that to happen, you need to lead them well all along.

I recommend the book "Employees First, Customers Second: Turning Conventional Management Upside Down" by Vineet Nayar to the reader.

Eventually, it is the leadership which sets the tone of the culture in the organization. We always look upon our parents, elders and bosses to act and behave like them. We get inspiration from these people, and when our foundation is firmly established in their company, that shapes our lives. If you practice honesty starting from home, we take this trait to the companies we work for. If we practice ethics, we will stand for these values, come what may.

As mentioned earlier, I cater to the MSME sector, and many need to be taught not only management systems, practices etc., but also these skills.

Here are the top qualities of leadership:

- **A leader knows the way and shows the way:**

Rather than saying "go", a leader should say "let's go."

- **He stands by his people:**

The leader has to coach, support and protect his people. He has to be in the line of fire first.

- **He should never fail on his promises made:**

But if he fails for whatever reason, he should have the courage to communicate clearly and set new goalposts.

The visionary and great leader Ratan Tata had promised to launch his Nano car for one lac rupees. It took years before the car was finally launched, and the costs had escalated by that time. Despite these challenges, he offered the first few cars for one lac and mentioned, "a promise is a promise."

- **A leader has to be a great visionary:**

When companies set the Big Audacious Hairy Goals (BHAG): A *BHAG*–pronounced "bee hag"–is a long-term goal that everyone in a company can understand and rally behind. It sounds crazy, but it's exciting and drives your people to believe in you. As a leader, if you cannot see this, your people will rarely see it.

- **Praise in front of others, but reprimand in private:**

This is a crucial trait many leaders need to carry. One cannot take undue advantage of your position and throw your weight around. As a leader, look for the most minor reason as a celebration point to motivate and inspire others. When reprimanding someone, make sure you are also a good listener before jumping to any conclusion.

- **Give credit to others and take the blame yourself:**

Giving credit speaks volumes of your character; when you put yourself in the firing line first, your people will step ahead for you. When projects are impossible to achieve, challenges are many, and deadlines are strict - these situations get the best of your people for you. Remember to back them up and give credit lavishly.

- **Stick to your values:**

There will be temptations where you can make some immediate benefits. Sometimes, you will be asked to compromise on your values. Leaders love these situations as they have to practice what they preach, and I urge readers to take advantage of these opportunities if they come across them.

Another aspect is of correcting your wrong decisions. You will be tested on your decision-making ability. In most cases in the MSME sector, particularly with fewer layers of management teams, the buck stops at the owner, and you may not always be equipped or right to take the apt decision. What matters when you realize the decisions have gone wrong is to call a spade a spade. You have to correct yourself, which will give the right message to your team.

I've encountered many situations in my career when I had to bite the bullet. I had to take unpopular decisions and stick to them. I have never worked to please my principals but always delivered in the interest of the task given. If my core values were asked to be compromised, if I could see my practices violated, I walked out of conference rooms without saying a word.

There have been cases where I have gracefully exited as there was no point convincing after a certain point. There were assignments when I challenged the owners in the Board rooms in front of others if I had observed unfair practices. My engagement ended with them, but the same people returned to me after a period and wanted to work with me again.

What does this tell you? As a leader, I practised what I believed in, which helps me continue today. I do not hold any grudge and have even walked off without getting paid, but the same people have offered work to me again, for they know what culture I belong to.

****

I've encountered many situations in my career when I had to bite the bullet. I had to take unpopular decisions and stick to them.

****

Questions to the reader:

Who are the leaders you look up to and why?

1.

2.

3.

4.

5.

What do these companies stand for in your mind? Does this reflect the culture of their company?

1. Amazon

2. Google

3. Infosys

4. The Tata Group

5. The Aditya Birla Group

6. Unilever

7. Reliance Industries

8. Godrej Group

9. Colgate

10. Zomato

11. Finally, your own Company:

Resources to use

Here are some handy resources that the reader can use for their benefit. These are pertaining to the industry in sectors of Consultancy, Training, Counselling, and Coaching.

A. https://reports.sourceglobalresearch.com/report/download/8942/extract/The-India-Consulting-Market-in-2022

This report covers extensively on the Indian Consulting market with trends, forecasts, functions in the consulting market etc.

B. https://www.infodesk.com/5-key-trends-in-2022-for-the-consulting-industry/consulting-industry/

It is always good to know the trends and what's in store. Here's something very informative on the professional service market.

C. https://www.reportlinker.com/market-report/Consulting/505091/Consulting/country/726396

The crucial market intelligence is what you will get from this report on a global scale.

D. https://linchpinseo.com/trends-in-the-management-consulting-industry/

Trends transforming the Management Consulting in 2023

These top ten trends and top ten statistics in management consulting will apprise you of the areas your consultancy must focus on to continually grow and land new clients.

The article covers:

1) Top 10 Trends

1.1) Continued Digitization

1.2) Legislation Shaping Business

1.3) Market Focus

1.4) Digital Integration

1.5) Fail Fast Methodology

1.6) Recruiting New Talent

1.7) Multi-sourcing Mode

1.8) Crowdsourced Talent

1.9) Consulting Firm Selection Process

1.10) Continued Education

E. https://blog.commlabindia.com/elearning-design/elearning-trends-2023

Online training is evolving, and so are the eLearning trends for 2023. Continue reading to find out the top 7 hottest L&D trends in 2023.

F. https://indianexpress.com/article/brand-initiative/demand-for-top-business-coaches-is-rising-in-india-8111023/

"The Indian coaching industry has shown strong resilience in the face of the pandemic, even after taking an initial hit. At a time when businesses were looking for ways to cut costs wherever they could, this new industry of coaching has shown to be impactful in helping many businesses".

References

Preface:

Marshall Goldsmith's book "What Got You Here, Won't Get You There"

https://marshallgoldsmith.com/book-page-what-got-you-here/

https://www.amazon.in/What-Got-Here-Wont-There/dp/0739342231

Zig Ziglar

https://www.ziglar.com/

https://en.wikipedia.org/wiki/Zig_Ziglar

See You at the Topby Zig Ziglar, Al Mayton (Illustrator)

https://www.goodreads.com/book/show/161415.See_You_at_the_Top

Father Agnel Engineering College

https://en.wikipedia.org/wiki/Fr._Agnel_Multipurpose_School_and_Junior_College

LAKSHYAVEDH Institute of Leadership & Excellence

https://lakshyavedh.com/

About the Author

Wai, Pune

https://www.nativeplanet.com/travel-guide/all-you-need-to-know-about-wai-maharashtra-003301.html

7 Habits of Highly Effective People" by Stephen Covey

https://www.franklincovey.com/the-7-habits/

https://www.amazon.com/Habits-Highly-Effective-People-Powerful/dp/0743269519

What is my role as a client? What am I expected to do?

The Theory Of Constraints

https://www.leanproduction.com/theory-of-constraints/#:~:text=The%20Theory%20of%20Constraints%20is,referred%20to%20as%20a%20bottleneck.

How did I become a Trainer?

7 Habits of Highly Effective People" by Stephen Covey

https://www.franklincovey.com/the-7-habits/

https://www.amazon.com/Habits-Highly-Effective-People-Powerful/dp/0743269519

Landmark

https://www.landmarkworldwide.com/

Zig Ziglar

https://www.ziglar.com/

https://en.wikipedia.org/wiki/Zig_Ziglar

How did I become a Counsellor?

Father Agnel Engineering College

https://en.wikipedia.org/wiki/Fr._Agnel Multipurpose_School_and_Junior_College

How did I become a Consultant?

Father Agnel Engineering College

https://en.wikipedia.org/wiki/Fr._Agnel_Multipurpose_School_and_Junior_College

LAKSHYAVEDH Institute of Leadership & Excellence

https://lakshyavedh.com/

3.30% Life Insurance penetration in India.

https://www.edelweisstokio.in/blogs/edelweiss-tokio-life/only-few-of-indias-population-is-covered-under-a-life-insurance-plan

My purpose which drives me all these years

Corient Business Solutions

https://corientbs.com

Good to Great by Jim Collins

https://www.jimcollins.com/article_topics/articles/good-to-great.html

https://www.amazon.com/Good-Great-Some-Companies-Others/dp/0066620996

The art of storytelling:

"Paap & Punya"

(https://en.wikipedia.org/wiki/Punya_(Hinduism)#:~:text=The%20Ny%C4%81ya%20School%20understands%20dharma,to%20well%2Dbeing%20and%20duty.)